Original title:
Leaves of the Living Room

Copyright © 2025 Creative Arts Management OÜ
All rights reserved.

Author: Tobias Winslow
ISBN HARDBACK: 978-1-80581-918-9
ISBN PAPERBACK: 978-1-80581-445-0
ISBN EBOOK: 978-1-80581-918-9

Clusters of Calm and Color

In corners bold, the greens collide,
With socks and shoes, they do reside.
The cat's now king, in plant parade,
His royal throne, a fern charade.

A spider spins a web of dreams,
While dust bunnies plot in moonbeam teams.
The couch giggles, the pillows sigh,
As mischief brews with a wary eye.

Potpourri whispers, scents so bright,
Jokes of lemony freshness take flight.
We laugh at the plants, they laugh at us,
In this quirky space, who needs to fuss?

So here's to greens, both wild and wise,
In goofy poses, with glinting eyes.
A room that breathes, with spirit and glee,
Come join the fun, it's where we're free!

The Lush Living Room Legacy

A rubber plant rocks a jazzy flare,
While succulents form a funky prayer.
The cushions dance, a wobbly groove,
In this leafy place, we find our move.

Recliners boast a leafy charm,
While vases sing, no need for harm.
The echo of laughter fills the air,
As vines and fabrics form a pair.

Stickers on pots, a quirky tale,
"Water me less!" they seem to wail.
However, they thrive, with silly pride,
In this comedy club, they take their stride.

So raise a glass to our green brigade,
Their funny antics, forever displayed.
In this cozy nook, where chaos reigns,
Ah, the charm of plants, and all their gains!

Heartbeat of the Hearth

In the nook where the couch hugs tight,
A fern named Ferny claims the light.
He sways and dances to the beat,
Who knew a plant could be so neat?

Chasing dust bunnies with grace so bold,
While the cat's ambition remains uncontrolled.
When guests arrive, they stand aghast,
At how Ferny plays, and they just laugh.

Botanicals in the Boudoir

In the boudoir, where dreams take flight,
Pothos climbs, a true delight.
Whispers secrets, tales to share,
As I doze off, it doesn't care.

The cactus pricks at my lazy aim,
While succulents play a leafy game.
A bromeliad tries to steal the show,
Swapping fashion tips with a rogue aloe.

Serenity in the Subtle Green

In corners green with a touch of whimsy,
Sits a peace lily, not very flimsy.
It nods to the rhythm of my TV's song,
While my knees crack loud, it still sings along.

With every laugh, its petals shake,
Even it knows when I'm awake.
A quiet witness to all my schemes,
In a world where nothing quite redeems.

Verses Among the Vines

Tangled trails of ivy twirl,
Like a dancer with a dizzy whirl.
They wrap around the lamp with glee,
Growing clumsy, oh what a spree!

The spider plant shimmies on sill,
Encouraging chaos with such strong will.
As I trip on my own two feet,
The vines decide to dance, so sweet!

Petals and Pledges

In a pot, a rogue fern sings,
It claims it owns the room's bright bling.
A mock tail made of shed green fluff,
Decorates the sofa, isn't that enough?

The cactus brags with prickly cheer,
It tickles the cat, a furry sneer.
While orchids waltz with graceful flair,
Spreading gossip throughout the air.

Harmony of Indoor Life

The rubber tree claims it's the king,
Waving its leaves like a golden ring.
Succulents gather for a gossip spree,
Murmurs about the dust on ol' Bambi.

The potted herbs have their own chat,
Complaining about a sneaky cat.
Basil says, 'I smell a big old rat!'
While rosemary just rolls on the mat.

The Heartbeat of Houseplants

Fern and spider plant in a dance,
Creating chaos, they take a chance.
Potting soil spills like confetti bright,
Every day feels like a party night.

The ivy stretches, trying to climb,
Competing with lizards, oh so sly.
"Who wore it better?" they laugh and bicker,
As sunlight leaves us all a little quicker.

Boughs Within the Walls

A potted palm acts like a non-stop fool,
Insisting it's the star of every duel.
While ferns do pirouettes on the floor,
A leafy praise for their wacky lore.

The peace lily rolls its eyes with glee,
"We're not just decor, we're family!"
Together they plot to pull a prank,
On the human who forgot to give thanks.

Sanctuary of Shadows and Serenity

A plant dressed in green, oh so bright,
It nods and it sways, quite a sight.
It whispers my secrets, no shame in its shade,
Who knew a ficus could be so well-played?

The sunlight streams in, a dance on the floor,
Petals are giggling, always wanting more.
I try to relax, but the cat thinks it's fun,
To pounce on the leaves — oh you silly bun!

Hearthside Hues of Nature

Cushions all sprawled with a vibrant flair,
A fern in the corner, it's giving me scare.
With every soft rustle, I jump and I squeal,
Nature's here creeping, oh what a deal!

The fish in their bowl are throwing a party,
While I chomp on snacks, feeling quite hearty.
This cozy abode, a wild yet tame show,
Who needs the great outdoors? I've got this flow!

Whispers in the Corner

In the quietest corner, a spider has spun,
It's hosting a gathering — come see the fun!
Each trim little leaf is a tag on the guest list,
But I hold my breath — do they know I'm a pest?

A cactus with quirks offers points of view,
But let's not offend Mr. Succulent too.
Amidst laughter and giggles, the plants have a ball,
Meanwhile, I'm left hoping they'll share with us all!

Green Shadows on the Wall

The shadows are dancing, the walls start to sway,
Every twist and each turn seems ready to play.
Why does the pothos look so full of sass?
I can't help but chuckle, it's got so much class!

An ivy vine giggles, with a glint in its eye,
As I tell my punchlines, it gives them a try.
A fountain of laughter where greenery grows,
This joke-loving jungle is everyone's knows!

The Hearth's Garden

In pots they dance, all green and bright,
Tiny leaves catch morning light.
A fern's whisper, a cactus grin,
Who knew the fun they'd bring within?

The cat plots moves, oh such a sight,
To prune the plants with all his might.
But they just laugh, it's all a game,
As he pounces, oh what a shame!

The tomato plant wears a crown of red,
While basil dreams of pizza in bed.
Sweet rosemary smirks, holding her own,
In this wild jungle, we've overgrown!

Of pots and plots, a leafy spree,
A living room with giggles and glee.
So if you ask what's nature's jig,
It's chaos disguised in a little fig!

Reflections of a Grown-Up Jungle

In corners lurk those leafy dreams,
A jungle thrives with quirk and schemes.
The rubber plant gives side-eye stares,
While spider plants spin fuzzy hairs.

Each shelf a stage, a leafy play,
Where sunlight bursts in a golden ray.
Pothos climbing, oh so spry,
As the dog just wonders, 'Why oh why?'

The philodendron starts to sway,
Dancing leaves in a cheerful way.
A cactus boasts of prickly fame,
While the ferns giggle at the game.

In this wild age, all plants take flight,
A grown-up jungle, oh what a sight!
With laughter echoing, plants unite,
Living it up in sheer delight!

Foliage Frames in a Cozy Nest

A frames of green, a cozy tale,
Where sunlight dances, soft as a veil.
Cherished pots in a snug embrace,
Bring a smile to every face.

An orchid sings as the dog runs wild,
While the parakeet watches, excited and riled.
The pothos creeps beyond the books,
A plant with secrets and playful hooks.

A clumsy cat trips over a base,
As if the plants are playing a race.
With every tumble and joyful fall,
They cheer each other, through it all.

These frames hold laughter, a silly view,
In a cozy nest where fun is true.
Every leaf a smile, every petal a jest,
In this leafy world, we're all guests!

Cozy Canopies of Home

Beneath the leaves, tranquility reigns,
A canopy of laughter, joy unchains.
Where plants conspire with playful glee,
Inviting antics, come and see!

The monster plant licks the curtain's hem,
While the little succulents watch the mayhem.
They giggle and snicker, roots intertwined,
In this home jungle, love's defined.

A rubber tree sounds a rubbery laugh,
As the goldfish plots its watery path.
Poppies dream of sunshine's kiss,
In this cozy abode, what bliss!

When dusk falls and the lights grow dim,
The plants form shadows, on a whim.
In cozy canopies, where mischief plays,
Home is where the laughter stays!

Verdant Reflections in Glass

In a corner a cat sits napping,
A fern's waving, all in good clapping.
On the shelf, a gnome snores loud,
While the cactus joins, quite proud.

The light casts shadows, a dance so spry,
Cupboard plants wink with an eye.
Silly green faces in potted rows,
Who knew plants could strike silly poses?

Relics of Roots and Repose

A rubber plant dons a bow tie,
While succulents giggle as they dry.
A spider plant swings from the ledge,
Playing tag with the edge of the hedge.

Mosses gossip in a giggly spree,
Telling tales of the last tea spree.
With every leaf that flutters around,
Roommates laugh at the click-clack sound.

Breath of the Emerald Embrace

In the sun's glow, shadows play,
Pothos whispers secrets of the day.
A leafy cheerleader roots for the couch,
While mismatched curtains grin, no slouch.

Green companions stand tall in delight,
All with a hint of mischief in sight.
Sipping sunlight like a quirky brew,
Who knows what they plan to pursue?

Delicate Dialogues of Dappled Light

A peace lily shakes, it's feeling fine,
When it hiccups, you know it's wine time!
A hanging ivy swings with glee,
While a jade plant says, 'Come talk to me!'

Wandering thoughts in a leafy debate,
Who can stretch longest while staying straight?
Chasing around a dust bunny's feint,
Laughing about being a clear saint!

Sheltered by Nature's Grace

In this green enclave, a squirrel's chase,
A fern's dance with dust in a peculiar space.
Potted plants gossip, sharing their tales,
While sunlight spills laughter, alive in the gales.

An ant in a hurry, on a mission so sly,
Dodges an easy chair, pondering why.
The cat in the corner, a king on a throne,
Dreams of the jungle, but he's never alone.

Plants play hide and seek, who's winning today?
They rustle with mischief in their leafy ballet.
A cactus rolls laughter, feeling quite tough,
While petunias whisper, 'We've had enough fluff!'

The Indoor Grove of Solitude

In shadows of solace, a plant breathes deep,
With secrets to share, while the humans all sleep.
Curled vines offer hugs, soft as a dream,
While curtains whisper gossip, a leafy regime.

A lizard takes charge, a tiny patrol,
Guarding the greenery, that's his main goal.
He trips on the mat, what a wobbly sight,
Raises his chin, 'I'm a knight, feeling bright!'

The rubber plant's pondering a trip to the sky,
Joking with ivy, who can't help but sigh.
'Just once, let's escape! A wild rendezvous!'
They chuckled and swayed, but what could they do?

Tides of Growth in Stillness

A potted palm dreams of waves and the breeze,
It flicks its green fingers, begging for peace.
The lilac is busy, plotting a bloom,
While dust bunnies gather, preparing for doom.

A spider spins tales on a gossamer thread,
Telling of journeys to far lands ahead.
While the daisy insists, 'We're just fine right here!'
In this pot of chaos, there's nothing to fear.

The snake plant's wise, it knows all too well,
Life's an odd mix of stories to sell.
So here we all linger, a quirky parade,
In our little green kingdom, we laugh and we fade.

Nature's Symphony in the Centerpiece

In the middle of chaos, a centerpiece sways,
Charmed by the laughter that fills up the bays.
A leaf rustles softly, 'Let's throw a bash!'
And the old vase chuckles, 'Oh, don't make a splash!'

A rogue little figure, a beetle on call,
Wants to dance on the table; oh, he's having a ball!
But the napkin protests, 'Aren't we too neat?'
'This party needs chaos, gumdrops, and feet!'

As snacks hit the ground, ants join the spree,
Forming a conga line, oh what a sight!
Each plant a witness, with wisdom to share,
To the wild, woven stories, in this fun-filled lair.

Harmonic Humidity

In corners where the ferns do dance,
They greet the guests with leafy prance.
The air is thick with jokes and cheer,
Who knew green friends had such a sphere?

The ivy chuckles, 'Come, have a seat!'
Whilst rubber plants hold a veggie meet.
Pothos twirls in the gentle breeze,
Trying to win with charming ease.

Cacti look on, all prick and pout,
'We are the kings, without a doubt!'
But the wilting flowers, in a flare,
Cry, 'We're the beauty, don't you dare!'

Around a light, the laughter blooms,
As sunlight filters, dispelling glooms.
Each plant a character, so quirky and bright,
In their leafy realm, all feels just right.

Growth in Stillness

In silence, plants plot their grand scheme,
While shadows play, they laugh and beam.
A spider plant tells tales of the rain,
Its babies giggle, not feeling pain.

The jade winks at the passing cat,
'Got your tail, it's now my mat!'
While peace lilies gossip, keeping it low,
Spilling secrets on who won the show.

Zebra plants strike a pose so grand,
As they sway gently, trying to stand.
'We take the crown of the cutest tile!'
While succulents snicker, 'We do it with style!'

Amidst the chaos, a calm prevails,
Nature's jesters wear green veils.
In the stillness, joy takes root,
In their grounded fun, life is a hoot.

Sanctuary of the Senses

In this green enclave, scents entwine,
A whiff of mint, oh so divine.
Herbs whisper secrets, so sweet and bright,
While sage chortles under soft moonlight.

The scent of damp earth makes the bark laugh,
As lilies chuckle in their soft path.
Basil's allure pulls everyone near,
Even the shy moss quivers with cheer.

If walls could giggle, they'd clap their hands,
Telling tales of moisture and sunny bands.
Every leaf, a jester, all in good fun,
Bringing delight till the day is done.

In this sanctuary, joy runs wild,
Each petal a joke, each stem a child.
A haven where laughter fills the air,
Plants in their humor, a charm so rare.

Tangles of Time and Tendrils

Twisting and turning, the vines do weave,
Creating a maze, oh can you believe?
With snickers and giggles, they twirl around,
As the world outside churns without a sound.

The trailing plant claims, 'I've got the flair,
To catch the light with nary a care.'
Meanwhile, the philodendron boasts its height,
Swaying like royalty, a regal sight.

In tangle and twist, friendships are made,
Each tendril's a party, never to fade.
Through verdant laughter, they grow with glee,
Creating a jungle, just you wait and see.

With roots intertwined, they toast to their fate,
In this curious world, there are no debates.
Time spins in circles, not a hurried race,
Among the greens, there's always a space.

Sunlight's Dance on Silk and Soil

In corners bright, where giggles bloom,
A pot of green brings cheer, not gloom.
The sunlight twirls on fabrics fine,
As soil whispers secrets, sweet as wine.

Chasing dust motes, the shadows prance,
A waltz with ferns in silly dance.
Potatoes peek with a cheeky grin,
While flowers chuckle, inviting kin.

Laughter weaves through vines so bold,
A tapestry of stories told.
With every branch a tale to share,
In this jungle, there's joy everywhere.

Stealthy cat in the sunlight sprawled,
With every rustle, she's enthralled.
Leaves shimmy, but hushed they stay,
As if in on the joke, they play.

Roots Beneath the Surface

Underneath the ground so sly,
Roots gossip daily, oh my, oh my!
They tickle dirt and swipe at bugs,
While moles host conferences with shrugs.

Knots and twists in a tangled heap,
Plotting their antics in silence deep.
Squirrels glance down, puzzled, bemused,
At this leafy world that's not confused.

Tap dance, tap dance, feel that beat,
The dance of roots beneath our feet.
Pulling pranks on worms and stones,
While every push brings silly groans.

Yet above, the branches sway,
Unaware of what's at play.
'Round the pot a game unfolds,
As rooty tales of mischief are told.

Symphony of Sprouts and Shadows

Sprouts break through in a cacao hue,
Each tiny leaf has plans to pursue.
They stretch and yawn with morning light,
While shadows hold their breath in fright.

A cacophony of giggles and squeaks,
As chirping crickets share their leaks.
Each poke of soil is filled with cheer,
Even old snails join the party near.

Conducting leaves like they were bands,
A breeze of laughter sways the stands.
With thumping roots and swirling buds,
The symphony plays in playful floods.

The sun takes bows, and shadows play,
As petals sip humidity's sway.
Foliage feasts on kindness grown,
A comedic gem in nature's throne.

The Folio of Flora

A book bound tight in green and gold,
With every page a story told.
Petals flutter, sharing glee,
While daisies wink, come read with me!

In chapters thick with leafy themes,
Twisting tales dance like crazy dreams.
The pothos charms with crafty lines,
While cacti holler wisdoms fine.

Each turn reveals a mischief plot,
The lilies debate, 'Is this the spot?'
With every turn, a laugh ignites,
In this merry world, all feels just right.

Pages rustle, a breeze does sing,
As laughter echoes from everything.
A folio open, wild and free,
What fun emerges when you peek and see!

Threads of Verdure in Living Spaces

In corners plants stand tall and proud,
Dressed in green, they laugh aloud.
Cacti wear a spiky crown,
While ferns just sway and never frown.

The rubber tree thinks it's a star,
While pothos clings and dreams of far.
Each leaf a story, each stem a joke,
As sunlight dances, laughter's evoked.

An ivy twist, a playful vine,
Wrapping the lamp, it claims it's fine.
"Oh watch me climb, I'm feeling spry!"
While grandma's gaze rolls with a sigh.

So gather 'round this leafy crew,
A comedy of greens in every hue.
In rooms where nature takes its stand,
Silly leaves make life so grand.

Nature's Canvas Adorned in Green

Abstract art hangs on the wall,
A fern with flair, it loves to sprawl.
A painter's easel takes a break,
To showcase greens, for goodness' sake!

The succulents hold a lively debate,
On who's the prettiest in their state.
They whisper secrets, oh what a contrive!
"Did you see me bloom? I'm quite alive!"

Hanging pots swing low and high,
Moss giggles softly, oh so shy.
As windows frame this artful scene,
Nature's mischief is always seen.

In the heart of homes, humor thrives,
Where every giggle of greenery strives.
To lift our spirits in lofty show,
With nature's brush, let the laughter flow.

The Cloistered Garden of Solace

A secret nook, so snug and neat,
Where potting soil and laughs do meet.
A thyme plant sings, a sage will chat,
As sunbeams tickle the old cat.

Pansies prank with faces bold,
While marigolds tell tales of old.
In this cloister of green delight,
Each little petal is a spark of light.

Basil dreams of pasta night,
While rosemary stands up for the fight.
Can you hear their funny banter here?
Amidst the greens, there's no room for fear.

So find your peace in this leafy realm,
Where giggling sprouts take at the helm.
In gardens sheltered from the stress,
Nature's humor can't help but impress.

Soft Leaves and Strong Lives

Soft leaves lounge upon the chair,
With tiny whispers in the air.
"Hey, buddy, what's your life like?"
"Still hanging, near the kitchen's spike."

The snake plant lies in glorious pose,
With one eye shut, it dozes and dozes.
While a spider plant dances with glee,
"Watch me jig; I'm wild and free!"

In pots where boredom dares to grow,
Greenery chuckles, "Here's the show!"
A bouncy bloom, a cheerful sprout,
Bringing joy with every shout.

Together they thrive, oh what a sight,
"Nobody's sad; our futures are bright!"
In living rooms, life's quirky dive,
Soft leaves and strong lives, all alive!

Tapestry of Tranquil Trellis

In a nook where sunlight plays,
A plant delights in leafy ways.
It twists and turns, a sprightly show,
Demanding snacks—just let it grow!

A jungle gym for dust and sweat,
Each branch a dare, a friendly bet.
The cat leaps high, in playful glee,
To catch a green intruder, whee!

Moss gathers dust where time forgot,
It laughs at us, does not care a jot.
We water it with half a grin,
While it thrives, we just take it on the chin!

So many greens upon the wall,
The finest friends, who heed the call.
With every sprout, a laugh bestowed,
In this room, the laughter flowed!

Foliage Dreams in the Parlor

A fern in the corner, sharp and chic,
Its leaves do waltz, so bold and sleek.
It dances round the table's edge,
Planning pranks—a leafy pledge!

A pothos climbs, it's quite the sight,
Chasing shadows in the night.
"Me? I'm just here for snacks," it shouts,
While gathering dust as laughter sprouts!

Bamboo bends, a comical gaze,
Spying on guests through a greenish haze.
It chuckles soft, with leaves that sway,
"Don't mind me, just here to play!"

A kaleidoscope of green so bright,
Turning drab days into pure delight.
In laughter's grip, we all unite,
With foliage dreams, our spirits take flight!

Resilience in the Urban Wilderness

Amid concrete jungles, brave and tough,
A plant stands firm, doesn't get rough.
With roots that grip through rock and grime,
It shrugs off troubles, one leafy rhyme!

Windows wide, it stretches tall,
Sipping sunshine—oh, what a ball!
The pigeons stare, can't believe their eyes,
As this green giant aims for the skies!

Underneath, the dustbunnies play,
Hiding shy from the leaves' array.
With every breeze, they spread the cheer,
Whispering secrets, drawing near!

So here we thrive, both charmed and bold,
With stories of laughter, yet untold.
In this wild dance, we forge and bloom,
Among the chaos, we find our room!

Eclipsed by Foliage

A trailing vine, a twist and twirl,
With every inch, it gives a whirl.
It wraps around, a leafy embrace,
Giggling softly, all over the place!

Sunlight sips through emerald green,
Turning the room to a comic scene.
It whispers whispers, tales they weave,
Oh, the mischief that one can achieve!

A cactus stands, in sharp repose,
Watching the antics of all that grows.
"Don't poke me!" it warns, with a grin,
While plants around it spin-spin-spin!

These green companions, quirky and spry,
Bring laughter forth, as days pass by.
Eclipsed by foliage, rampantly free,
In this wild haven, joy's decree!

Interludes of Ivy and Peace

Ivy drapes like a silly scarf,
Hiding chaos with a playful laugh.
In corners where the dust bunnies play,
Waging wars on socks gone astray.

Potted plants in a dance of cheer,
Each one whispering, "I'm happy here!"
A jungle of joy in a world so neat,
Where peace and mischief comically meet.

Laughter hides in each green fold,
With stories of sunlight and dirt retold.
When a leaf falls, it tells a joke,
Pulling smiles from the mundane cloak.

Chaos tumbles, and yet we find,
A symphony of nature, sweetly unlined.
With ivy as our heart's silly muse,
Life's comedy makes us light our blues.

Seedlings of Comfort Amidst Clutter

In a mess, seedlings sprout with glee,
Playing hide and seek, so carefree.
Amidst old toys and laundry piles,
They peek out with cheeky smiles.

Cactus in the corner says, "Don't poke!"
While rubber plants whisper tired jokes.
The mix of chaos in every pot,
Turns cluttered spaces into a sweet spot.

Ferns flop over like they're on break,
Plopping down for a giggle and shake.
A gentle tug of the messy thread,
All while chuckling, 'Let's make a bed!'

With every sprout, merriment grows,
In this cozy nook, our laughter flows.
Comfort found where the wild things wander,
In chaos blooms, we laugh and ponder.

Veils of Verdancy in Everyday Life

A curtain of green flutters and sways,
Hiding dust bunnies from day to day.
With each gentle breeze, it starts to tease,
These plants sure know how to make us freeze.

In corners a fern gives a cheeky flare,
Whispering secrets of the living air.
With pots like hats, adorned with grace,
They wiggle happily in their snug space.

The rubber tree, with a grin so wide,
Sways to rhythms of the sofa's side.
Little sprouts in the kitchen glow,
Brew up laughter where the spices flow.

So veils of green in our daily show,
Turn dull moments to a vibrant glow.
A world where nature does a jig,
Turning life's quirks into a playful gig.

When Nature Meets a Cozy Corner

When nature finds a cozy nook,
It tells old tales like an open book.
Cuddled in cushions, the vining plays,
As shadows dance in the morning rays.

The potted pals, with mismatched pots,
Tell the story of forget-me-nots.
In a corner where twinkling lights twirl,
They giggle and jive, a leafy swirl.

A cheeky sprout pranks the lamp's glow,
Flickering lights saying, "Look at me, though!"
Nature's whisper in a playful dance,
Plants tease our hearts, given the chance.

So here's to corners where plants indulge,
Turning our lives into a festive bulge.
A slice of green with humor and cheer,
Where friendship blossoms, bright and dear.

Nature's Whispers Between Walls

In the corner, a fern takes a seat,
It's plotting a dance with my old, worn feet.
The sunbeams giggle, what a sight to behold,
As shadows stretch out, daring the bold.

The spider spins tales, a webbed little mess,
While the potplant snores, no care for finesse.
A cactus is grumpy, it rarely gets hugs,
But still offers shade from those pesky old bugs.

Fish in their bowl, just circling around,
Arguing over who's the king of this ground.
The cat leaps and pounces, a knight in the night,
Yet all the green critters just giggle in fright.

So let's raise a toast, to the riot inside,
Where nature's found laughter, and plants take a ride.
With whispers of madness behind every book,
Here's to our jungle, come take a look!

Reflections of Resilience in Blossoms

In a vase on the table, blooms start to conspire,
With petals so bright, they aim to inspire.
A daisy winks at a shy little rose,
While the tulips gossip about their best clothes.

The sunflower leans in, with a grin on its face,
"Why don't you two join me, it's a wondrous place!"
But lilies disdain them, all haughty and tall,
Claiming their beauty should stand as the call.

A humble bouquet sprouts laughter and cheer,
"Stop comparing, dear friends, it's not why we're here!"
With colors so vibrant, they each find a way,
To dance through the sunlight and brighten the day.

So here in the room, where flowers can play,
They laugh and they banter, come what may.
And nature reminds us, in all of its schemes,
In unity blossoms, like friendship in dreams.

Sentinels of Serenity

Guardians of peace, the ferns stand so tall,
Meming the air with their calm, breezy thrall.
While the edges of pots hold secrets untold,
Of journeys the leaves took, their stories unfold.

In the sill of the window, a cactus declares,
"Step back, little critters, I'm armed with my prayers!"
With spines like swordfish, it's ready to fight,
While succulents chuckle, enjoying the light.

Oh, the timid bamboo sways gracefully slow,
Whispering tales of the world down below.
"Life's all in the sway, no reason to rush,
Just take it all in, let the heart feel the hush."

So here in this haven, where laughter takes wing,
Each plant with its charm, like the songs that they sing.
A chorus of nature that tickles the seams,
In the silence, they crash, like the wildest of dreams.

Humble Retreats of Green

Nestled in corners, the greens take a nap,
Wearing their leaves like a cozy old cap.
A little jade plant dreams of worlds far away,
While friends tease and giggle, in their leafy ballet.

The pothos hangs down, with a dramatic flair,
Saying, "Look at me! I'm the star of this lair!"
But the snake plant winks, a sage and a guide,
"In the humblest homes, we wear leafy pride."

A rubber plant struts, all shiny and bright,
While the peace lily nods, embracing the light.
"Don't forget the dracaena, always so wise,
It knows all the gossip behind its green guise."

So toast to the chaos, in pots and in soil,
To friendships that flourish, and hearts that uncoil.
In this retreat, laughter's in every seam,
Among humble retreats, we create a grand dream.

A Sanctuary in Petals and Cast Shadows

In the corner sits a plant, just so,
It thrives on whispers, and tales of woe.
With a pot that's chipped, it wears a grin,
Each leaf a secret, where shall we begin?

A spider creeps, in search of a snack,
While sunlight winks through leaves that slack.
Who knew these greens had such charm to wield?
They chatter and gossip, it's a leafy field.

A cat on the prowl, with curious eyes,
Thinks the fern could make a tasty prize.
But the foliage laughs, as it sways with cheer,
It's a jungle of laughter, nothing to fear.

So join the dance, of roots and fun,
In this home, the greenery has begun
To rule the roost and tickle the soul,
In petals and shadows, they take their toll.

Domestic Greenery's Sweet Surrender

In the sunshine, plants hold court,
With cheerful leaves that never thwart.
They sip the light, like a fine champagne,
Basking in glory, feeling no pain.

A cactus grins, with spikes in tow,
While daisies wink, putting on a show.
Each day a party, with soil and sun,
Who knew that plants could have such fun?

A fern is prancing, swaying around,
It seems to dance to a silent sound.
From potted pals to climbing vines,
In this green haven, joy intertwines.

So come and join the botanical spree,
With laughter blooming, wild and free.
Together we'll toast, with leaf and delight,
In this garden of humor, everything's right.

The Hidden Garden Within

Behind the curtain, a tapestry grows,
With unwritten stories that everyone knows.
A rubber tree whispers, 'What's next in line?'
While a rogue pothos dines on old sunshine.

The shelf is a stage, for all things green,
With little green friends, quite the scene.
As dust bunnies hop, under the chair,
The plants play hide-and-seek without a care.

The tongue plant teases, 'I'm tough, you see!'
But falls into laughter, as it spills its tea.
In this cozy nook, life bustles and beams,
Where every corner hosts mossy dreams.

So lift your cup to the flora around,
With each petal a giggle, in joy profound.
In this hidden garden, what magic thrives,
It's a world of whimsy where humor survives.

Parenting a Pot of Green

A tiny pot with dreams of grand,
I talk to it like it understands.
With water and love, we share our tales,
Oh, parenting plants, it never fails.

Little leaves sprout, defying the odds,
I cheer on their growth, giving applauds.
'You're doing great!' I say with pride,
While a snail moves slow, trying to hide.

Fingers crossed for blooms, that's the hope,
With fertilizer, I'm crafting a slope.
Each tiny shoot, a moment to cherish,
In this green circus, no joy shall perish.

So let's raise our glasses to flora divine,
In soil and sunlight, their struggles align.
Together we laugh, through thick and thin,
In this pot of green, we all win.

Echoes of the Wild in the Hearth

In the corner, a fern has grown,
Wearing a hat that was left alone.
It nods and sways with paint-patch grace,
As if it knows it's in a race.

A cactus grins, wearing spiky glee,
Pretending to be as soft as a pea.
It tells the tales of the dust bunnies,
Who plot their mischief; oh, so funny!

The ivy chuckles, creeping near,
Whispering secrets, oh so dear.
It claims to stretch to a great big plan,
To take over more space — a true green fan!

A palm tree dances with festive flair,
Mimicking moves that fill the air.
The dog looks on, with a confused glance,
Wondering if he should join the dance.

Lush Vignettes by the Window

A spider plant hangs, swaying with pride,
Joking with sunlight, "I'm your guide!"
It shared a wink with a bowl of fruit,
Who replied, "Hey, don't let me lose my loot!"

The pothos spills like a lazy stream,
Cheering the sun, "You're a real dream!"
A nearby chair can barely contain,
The laughter echoing through the pane.

Chubby leaves giggle, soft like pie,
Telling the couch, "Oh my, oh my!"
They toss around thoughts, a jumbled mess,
Swiftly debating which looks the best.

The curtain sways, with a playful tease,
Adding to this leafy unease.
A perfect stage for a plant-based play,
Where neighbors tune in to see who'll stay.

Silent Conversation with the Green

In the pot, the basil begins to plot,
With rosemary joining, quite the hotshot.
They whisper about what to spice the stew,
And giggle at memories of grass in dew.

A succulent sits, quite still and neat,
Taunting the dirt with its fancy seat.
It says, "I thrive on neglect and flair,
While you get swept like the dust in despair!"

Behind the curtain, the ferns connive,
Plotting their takeover, feeling alive.
"Let's shimmy the shelf and steal the show,
We'll have them laughing — oh, don't you know?"

Green paws wave to the couch, "Don't ignore!
Your fabric hides tales of pine and more."
What a riot, a leafy scene,
Where silence speaks louder among the green!

Paradise on the Shelf

Up on the shelf sits a giddy plant,
Dressed in soil, it starts to chant.
"Come gather around, let's have some fun,
I'll tell you tales till the day is done!"

A fern in the back rolls its leafy eyes,
"Will you please keep it down, oh wise one? Why?"
But the sunlight beams in, lighting the space,
Sending giggles around — it's a silly race!

A little sprout brags, "I'm the best in town,
While you're still waiting for your crown!"
The others chuckle, their roots intertwined,
In this jubilant chaos, they're perfectly aligned.

Soon all gather, from vine to stalk,
Sharing news with a leafy talk.
Near the window, their laughter swells,
A paradise wrapped in nature's spells.

Whispers of the Indoor Grove

In the corner, plants are peeking,
With a glimpse of green, they're speaking.
Are they plotting, oh so sly?
To make my cat jump and fly!

Tiny leaves, they gossip loud,
Chasing sunbeams, feeling proud.
A dance party on the sill,
As shadows stretch, they thrill and chill.

Potted friends with secrets bold,
Tales of mischief yet untold.
Have they seen the toast I burned?
Or how my houseplant wisdom turned?

I swear they laugh when I'm away,
Imagining what they might say.
A ruckus in the indoor cheer,
When it's just me, and they are near!

The Green Embrace Within

A jungle here in my small space,
With ferns that seem to take up space.
Do they argue or just conspire?
To reclaim my favorite chair and tire!

Spots of green with antics wide,
A leafy head, I now must hide.
They snicker when I bring the broom,
To tidy up their lovely room.

Are they plotting a leafy coup?
To turn my blender green, who knew?
Glancing sideways, oh so sly,
Are they laughing as I sigh?

In my heart, they bring the sun,
With humor woven into fun.
The greener the vibe, the louder the cheer,
My indoor grove fills me with queer!

Secrets in the Silhouette

Amidst the shadows, secrets twirl,
With hints of green, they inter swirl.
Whispers float in the evening light,
As plants plan parties out of sight!

Rubbery leaves play poker night,
Joking over a lack of fright.
One sly fern flips a card, you see,
Who knew it had such strategy?

The succulents are quite the crew,
Sipping water like it's brew.
While vines swing like they're on a ride,
Creating chaos, oh what a tide!

These silhouettes, they play pretend,
In their stories, I can't amend.
Roaring laughter in every leaf,
I join their fun, with zero grief!

Ferns in the Cozy Corner

In the corner, ferns convene,
Having tea, what a scene!
They giggle at my clumsy step,
As I vow my socks to prep.

Rugged greens, with jokes galore,
They've seen my wild dance floor.
Should I ask for a partner, though?
They wink and sway, stealing the show!

Houseplants thrive on every scheme,
Turning sunlight into cream.
With pots and soil their favorite toys,
Making mischief, oh what joys!

Ferns, you jest in wild delight,
Chatting away into the night.
With laughter bouncing off the wall,
My cozy corner hosts them all!

Garden Gossip Between the Walls

Two ferns gossip, oh what a sight,
About the cat who gives them a fright.
A spider claims he knows it all,
While the cactus rolls his eyes, oh so small.

Pothos peeks 'round the corner sly,
While the peace lily gives a dreamy sigh.
Each whisper floats through the room,
Creating a floral, funny bloom.

The Art of Indoor Greenery

A potted plant paints with a wink,
While the ivy tries to out-think.
Cacti compete in a prickly race,
As succulents smile with a sunny face.

The dracaena shows off her flair,
Prancing like she just doesn't care.
Fern fronds wave as if to say,
'Who needs sunlight when you can sway?'

Flourishing Spirits Attached to Soil

A rubber plant tells tales of rain,
While basil counts the drops of pain.
Fiddles laugh, green leaves ablaze,
With stories of playful, plant-filled days.

Herbs in the kitchen, a riotous scene,
Argue over who's the best cuisine.
Thyme rolls its eyes in spice-filled glee,
Saying, 'I'm the star, just wait and see!'

Portraits of the Verdant Kind

A family photo on the shelf,
The monstera mocks, 'I'm quite the elf!'
Potted pals pose for the show,
Each with personalities that glow.

Chlorophytum claims it roots for fame,
While snake plants play their own proud game.
In this gallery of quirky charms,
Living art that always warms.

Sun-Kissed Leaves in the Lounge

Sunlight dances, what a sight,
Plants pirouette, feeling bright.
A fern whispers, 'What's the tea?'
While cacti grin, full of glee.

Pots on shelves, a leafy squad,
Joking softly, 'Ain't it odd?'
Succulents roll their beady eyes,
'We're the kings of cozy lies.'

A spider plant throws a party,
In its strands, it feels quite hearty.
'Who needs soil?' the ivy quips,
While roses roll their paper lips.

In this jungle, laugh and cheer,
Every plant has jokes to share.
So come and join the leafy spree,
In this lounge, we're wild and free.

Homespun Nature's Chorus

In the nook where sunlight beams,
Green companions fulfill dreams.
Rubber plant sings: 'Join my band!'
With every note, they take a stand.

Pothos drapes with flair and glee,
'Green is the new black, can't you see?'
A peace lily winks, 'What's the scoop?'
While ferns gossip with a swoop.

Herbs in pots, a fragrant show,
Basil bursts with cheeky flow.
'Chives are great, but I'm the star!'
They argue who is best, by far.

Beneath the sun, they thrive and laugh,
Nature's joy, a perfect craft.
Tales of growth in every sprout,
In this room, let laughter shout!

The Color of Domestic Wilderness

Potted treasures, bright and bold,
Whisper secrets, tales retold.
'What if we could walk?' they jest,
Cacti nod; they know what's best.

In this patch of wild delight,
A rubber tree takes flight.
'I'm a hero, fear my leaves!'
As moss sneers, 'Yeah, wear your sleeves!'

The snake plant calls, with cheeky flair,
'In this home, we rule the air!'
Creeping vines join in the fun,
Twisting tales like they've just spun.

With every frond, a joke to share,
In a world that's filled with care.
Laughter echoes, bold and free,
In this space, just you and me.

Serenity in Every Sprout

In a corner, green and bright,
Houseplants giggle, pure delight.
'Who needs flowers?' one plant quips,
'Our charm alone makes hearts do flips.'

A tiny sprout, with pride it beams,
'I'm growing fast; I live the dreams!'
While ferns argue over who's more wise,
Banter echoes, filling the skies.

Each shelf adorned, a leafy façade,
Together they form a leafy squad.
'Who's thirsty?' yells the parlor palm,
In the chaos, there's such a calm.

So here we gather, blooms and puns,
In nature's arms, we've just begun.
Life is a jest, with roots so grand,
Join the laughter, hand in hand!

Serenity Among the Stems

In the corner, a green thumb thrives,
Potted pals with comical jives.
They wave and sway, a leafy ballet,
As sunlight spills out in a playful ray.

Chlorophyll giggles on a sunny day,
With each new sprout, they frolic and play.
Silently thriving, they chuckle and tease,
Bantering softly with the gentle breeze.

An ancient fern gives wisdom a nod,
While cacti poke fun, feeling quite broad.
Succulents smirk in their sunny embrace,
Reminding each other of their cozy space.

Here, serenity dances, leafy and bright,
In this quirky haven, they bask in delight.
Laughter resounds through photosynthetic cheer,
A household of humor, no worries here!

Urban Eden in Sunlight's Glare

Amidst the concrete, a jungle thrives,
Urban emeralds with humor in their lives.
A rubber plant tells tales of the street,
While spider plants pirouette to the beat.

Windows aglow with dazzling delight,
Sun-loving greens bask in the bright.
A cactus and fern share giggles anew,
Playing peek-a-boo in their leafy zoo.

A vine starts to climb, oh such a climb,
Hilarious attempts at their growth over time.
Wisteria whispers secrets from above,
While ferns give side-eyes to all with love.

In this urban haven, fun takes flight,
With antics and laughter, they feel just right.
Each plant has its story, each pet grows dear,
Life's an adventure, so let's all cheer!

The Dance of the Dusty Leaves

In sunlight's glow, they swirl and twirl,
A quirky dance, oh what a whirl!
Dusty leaves laugh as they glide,
In a comedic ballet, side by side.

With each gust of wind, a twist and a shout,
What a hilarious air, flipping about.
A tumble here and a spin there too,
These leaves know how to steal a view.

They giggle and rustle, a fluttering tune,
As shadows play tricks with the afternoon.
Each pirouette, a comic reprise,
Tickling the air, to all our surprise.

So as they sway in the light's warm embrace,
Join the laughter, find your own place.
For in this dance, humor's always found,
Among dusty leaves, joy knows no bound!

Green Guardians of the Living Space

Nestled and nurtured in every nook,
These green guardians offer their look.
With eyes of jade, they watch and they grin,
Guarding the laughter that bubbles within.

A mischievous pothos, sly and spry,
Hiding in shadows, just watching you try.
While a monstrous monstera plays peek-a-boo,
Winking at guests, it secretly knew.

Sprawled on the sill, the daisies conspire,
Telling each other their latest desire.
With every bloom, they chuckle in glee,
In this funny family, just wait and see.

In bright living rooms full of delight,
These green beings bring laughter day and night.
So raise your glass to these cherished greens,
For in their presence, life's full of scenes!

The Sanctuary of Verdant Dreams

In a corner, green wonders sprout,
Ferns whisper secrets, they never shout.
Cacti declare with prickly charm,
While ivy plays hide and seek, no harm.

Each leaf has a tale, a comical lore,
Of how it danced when the breeze hit the door.
Succulents chuckle, their humor is dry,
Next to them, forgetting, the ribbons of rye.

A technicolor jungle in mismatched pots,
Conversations held between tiny knots.
When guests come to visit, they nod and smile,
While the potted crew plots to stay awhile.

In this leafy haven, joy will not cease,
Where laughter grows thicker, a green masterpiece.
Join the fun, lets paint the walls bright,
In this whimsical realm, all's just right!

Whispered Breath of Nature's Kin

Chattering leaves in their cozy retreat,
Eavesdrop on stories while sipping fresh tea.
Pineapple plants prance in pattered delight,
While ferns wiggle and giggle, quite a sight.

Spider plants tease with their nimble twirl,
As rubber trees strut, giving everyone a whirl.
Tropical pals play bingo with sun,
Winning a glance, oh, isn't this fun?

In daylight they dance, when the humans are near,
At night, they conspire, but never show fear.
Sprinklers play tunes that they do adore,
Swaying to rhythms of life evermore.

Happiness blossoms where laughter is found,
Echoing softly, the giggles abound.
Join in the jest, bring your own grin,
In this lively boutique where the fun won't thin!

Potted Poems of the Domestic Jungle

Nestled with care, they bask in the light,
Each pot a chapter, in green, pure delight.
Cacti pen poems in prickles of glee,
While flowers compose with a hint of esprit.

Orchids wear hats fit for a fancy soirée,
Witty remarks in the flower display.
Tales of their travels on breezes we share,
As succulents snicker, no worry, no care.

They write of the sun's warm and loving embrace,
And moonlit adventures in their leafy space.
With soil as their canvas, they flourish and thrive,
In a world full of laughter, they come alive.

Every leaf a quip, every stem a jest,
In this verdant haven, they blossom the best.
So come take a look, bring your joyful heart,
For in this domestic jungle, the fun's just the start!

The Essence of Green Growth

A riot of colors where hilarity blooms,
Potted pals plotting, crafting their tunes.
Vines twirl and whirl with jest in their sway,
As humor crawls free in a leafy ballet.

Green giants chuckle in silence profound,
While orchids remind us laughter's a sound.
Bamboo whispers wisdom, peculiar but right,
In this garden of giggles, hearts take flight.

Sunlight and laughter, they harmoniously blend,
Drawing in smiles that twist and unbend.
Join in the merriment, let spirits collide,
In this enchanting space where good cheer does reside.

The essence of growth is not just the green,
It's giggles and joy, a sight to be seen.
So linger a while in this nurturing glen,
For nature's a comrade, a funny old friend!

Echoes of the Indoor Orchard

In the corner, a cactus waves,
Wishing it could be on brave knaves.
Palm fronds gossip about the breeze,
While potting soil just aims to please.

Spider plants plot a little dance,
In their small pots, they crop and prance.
A fern keeps secrets from the light,
Now that's a leafy oversight!

Succulents grumble, feeling so small,
While the rubber plant stands tall.
They share their dreams of trips to sun,
Imagining green escapes would be fun!

But when the vacuum zooms around,
They freeze, as if on hallowed ground.
Yet when it's quiet, what a sight,
They cheer for life, these greens so bright!

The Quiet Revolt of Greenery

In the shadows, ferns start to grumble,
While ivy on the shelf begins to fumble.
The basil winks, trying to sprout,
"Let's conquer this room! Let's kick it out!"

Potted pals roll their little leaves,
Planning mischief as the sunlight weaves.
A rogue thyme daringly takes the stage,
"Let's spice it up, let's engage!"

Orchids laugh, wrapped in their charm,
While a rubber plant puts up an arm.
"Who needs sunlight? We'll just pretend,
To grow like legends, we will ascend!"

Then comes the day the cat steps by,
Knocking down dreams with just one try.
With a leaf or two left in dismay,
The plants unite, "We've had our play!"

Windowsill Reveries

On the sill, a jade plant yawns,
Daring sun to wake at dawns.
A cactus dreams of snowflake tunes,
While ivy croons under the moons.

"Do you think it's time to chat?"
Said the orchid, wearing a hat.
"Let's swap stories of the past,
Of breezes warm and moments vast!"

Sage offers wisdom, fresh and bold,
While the fern claims it's never old.
They sip on sunshine, sprout some glee,
Living legends, wild and free!

Then the dog slips, oh, what a mess!
Potting soil now is in distress!
But still they laugh, with love in tow,
For stories bloom wherever they grow!

Room for Botanicals

In the corners, trouble brews,
Plant pots hug the bright blue hues.
"Who lives where?" they tug and tease,
In every nook, they plant the keys.

A snake plant ponders its next plan,
While a palm dreams of being a fan.
"Let me sway, let me twirl around,
I'll draw more love from the ground!"

But when the dog darts past the vase,
All the whispers turn to a chase.
Foliage flails, it's quite the sight,
Each leaf clings tight, oh what a fright!

Yet as the sun dips low in the room,
They settle down, forgetting the gloom.
For tomorrow brings another chance,
For fun and triumph, and a little dance!

Ethereal Echoes of Green Shades

In corners they giggle, the ferns dance,
The sofa seems jealous, not taking a chance.
Sunbeams sneak in to tickle their cheeks,
As pet cats plot mischief, their antics unique.

Picture a cactus, with pride and with sway,
Imitating statues, no words left to say.
While rubber plants whisper, sharing their dreams,
Of winning a trophy for funniest themes.

A Symphony of Silken Fronds

Chlorophyll choruses play soft in the breeze,
A fiddle leaf fig serenades with such ease.
The pothos performs with dramatic flair,
As dust bunnies giggle from under the chair.

The spider plant's children hang down like a show,
Pretending to juggle while putting on a low.
Green thumbs applaud from the audience space,
While squirrels in the window start comically race.

Vivid Botanicals in Indoor Repose

Succulents snicker, their shapes all askew,
They poke fun at daisies, a colorful crew.
Pansies are plotting to start a big fight,
While basil insists it can season with spite.

A fern whispers secrets to the curious sage,
As laughter erupts from the well-worn page.
They strive for a role in the next outdoor play,
But for now, they're cozy, in their potting display.

The Understory of Domestic Life

Amidst the loud chatter, the ivy sprawls wide,
Critiquing the antics of guests and their pride.
An orchid rolls eyes at a dusty old frame,
While peeking out shyly, avoiding the fame.

A rubber plant grins, it's seen quite a show,
It holds all the journals and tales from below.
With branches entwined in a humorous snare,
They laugh at the chaos that fills up the air.

Sunlit Shadows of Serenity

In corners where the sunlight beams,
Dust bunnies dance in leafy dreams.
A cactus tickles with a grin,
While spider plants plot to take skin.

The fern whispers jokes to the chair,
While succulents gossip without a care.
I swear my peace lily rolled its eyes,
When I forgot its weekly prize.

Each petal flickers, a secret spy,
Keeping tabs on the couch and why.
A watering can's a knight in plight,
Saving green friends from day to night.

In this lush hideaway so spry,
Even my rubber plant is sly.
It stretches lazily, taking a nap,
Dreaming of dirt and the gardener's map.

The Lush Hideaway

Beneath the shelf where books lay flat,
A philodendron holds a chat.
Its vines unravel like tales so bold,
While the bookshelf silently grows old.

A pot of basil, a fragrant trick,
Whispers recipes, fast and quick.
Mint laughs as it flutters around,
While my poor coffee plant just frowns.

A sunflower stands, in all its flare,
Making the others feel quite bare.
Yet everyone knows, so sweet, so spry,
The rubber tree just won't comply.

If you peek, do not be shy,
You'll find the secrets that plants reply.
A puddle of laughter, it's plain to see,
In my little lair, oh what glee!

Solace in the Potted Paradise

In pots adorned with patterns so bright,
My leafy crew brings pure delight.
A golden path where sunlight spills,
Makes each plant dance with joyful thrills.

A ribbon plant twirls with glee,
It knows the difference between you and me.
A tiny sprout, so fresh and spry,
Waves hello as I rush by.

The spider plant strums its lazy tune,
While hanging vines begin to swoon.
Every leaf has a silly tale,
Of garden adventures, they'll regale.

In this snug nook where laughter thrives,
Plant-based giggles make bright lives.
My home, a stage, where all can play,
In this potted paradise, come what may!

Nature's Canvas at Twilight

As dusk descends with a playful jig,
A jade plant dons a tiny wig.
Hiding secrets, it rolls its eyes,
Under the glow of growing skies.

The peace lily chuckles, soft and sweet,
While the rubber plant finds its feet.
An orchestra of pots begins to hum,
With melodies of laughter before the numb.

Outside the window, shadows blend,
Plant silhouettes become my friends.
Together they plot a silly scheme,
For a garden party, a leafy dream.

Nature, a canvas with textures bright,
Paints each corner with soft twilight.
In this tranquil mess, I sit and grin,
As my vibrant plants begin to spin!

The Fern's Lament

In a pot, I sit and sway,
Dreaming of the outdoor play.
One day I'll stretch my fronds so wide,
But nah, I'll nap and bide my pride.

The sunbeams tease, they start to gleam,
But here I am, a silent dream.
My friends, the dust bunnies, laugh so loud,
While I just frown, feeling so proud.

Each time you water, I can't help split,
My roots may quake, but I won't quit.
I'll grow tall and green without a curse,
Just spare a thought, don't make it worse.

In this cozy nook, I find my place,
Just don't forget to dust my face.
A fussy fern needs love and care,
Or I might just start to shed despair.

Secrets of the Potted Oasis

Tiny pots stacked up so high,
Whispers of the soil, oh my!
Gather 'round, let's start a show,
Each leaf has tales we want to know.

Garden gnome, stop telling lies,
Saying that we watch the skies.
We're just here, in jungle dreams,
Plotting how to steal the screams.

The cat walks past, we give a cheer,
'Oh look! Another brave soul here!'
If they only knew our giggly plot,
To take their space, oh, like it or not!

Beware the vacuum, it roars so loud,
It scares the joy from every shroud.
But when it's still, we'll sing and sway,
In our potted haven, we dance and play.

Nature's Embrace within Four Walls

A trampoline of leaves, we bounce with cheer,
Nature's party – come one, come near!
The couch is soft, the light is dim,
And here's where our laughter's brim.

Dusty corners, cobweb art,
A leafy heart that's set apart.
We twirl and spin on windowsills,
Creating chaos but with our thrills.

The cat claims a throne, so regal and proud,
While we scheme far beneath the cloud.
Snagging sunlight, that's our prime,
In this green kingdom, we live in rhyme.

Beneath these walls, life hums a tune,
A fine mix of green and a bit of cartoon.
So pull up a chair, let's have a brew,
In this quirky space, all's shiny and new!

The Indoor Canopy's Breath

Up above, the leafy shroud,
Whispers secrets, always loud.
'What's for lunch?' the plants discuss,
While I just sit, feeling nonplussed.

On a sunny day, I try to bake,
But plants say no, for goodness' sake!
'Don't let the heat make us all wilt,'
So I allow them their leafy quilt.

A jungle gym of vines galore,
Swinging fun – that's my décor.
With coffee spills, it's all a mess,
But hey, who needs to impress?

We dance when the wind starts to blow,
Indoor breezes are quite the show.
With giggles and hops, we flourish and breathe,
In the midst of chaos, we find relief.

www.ingramcontent.com/pod-product-compliance
Lightning Source LLC
Chambersburg PA
CBHW070309120526
44590CB00017B/2599